AH-1W
SUPER COBRAS

BY DENNY VON FINN

EPIC

BELLWETHER MEDIA · MINNEAPOLIS, MN

EPIC BOOKS are no ordinary books. They burst with intense action, high-speed heroics, and shadows of the unknown. Are you ready for an Epic adventure?

This edition first published in 2013 by Bellwether Media, Inc.

No part of this publication may be reproduced in whole or in part without written permission of the publisher. For information regarding permission, write to Bellwether Media, Inc., Attention: Permissions Department, 5357 Penn Avenue South, Minneapolis, MN 55419.

Library of Congress Cataloging-in-Publication Data

Von Finn, Denny.
AH-1W Super Cobras / by Denny Von Finn.
    p. cm. – (Epic books: military vehicles)
Includes bibliographical references and index.
Audience: Ages 6-12.
Summary: "Engaging images accompany information about AH-1W Super Cobras. The combination of high-interest subject matter and light text is intended for students in grades 2 through 7"–Provided by publisher.
ISBN 978-1-60014-815-6 (hbk. : alk. paper)
  1. HueyCobra (Helicopter)–Juvenile literature. I. Title.
UG1233.A459 2013
623.74'63–dc23   2012002391

Printed in the United States of America, North Mankato, MN.

A special thanks to Ted Carlson/Fotodynamics for contributing images.

TABLE OF CONTENTS

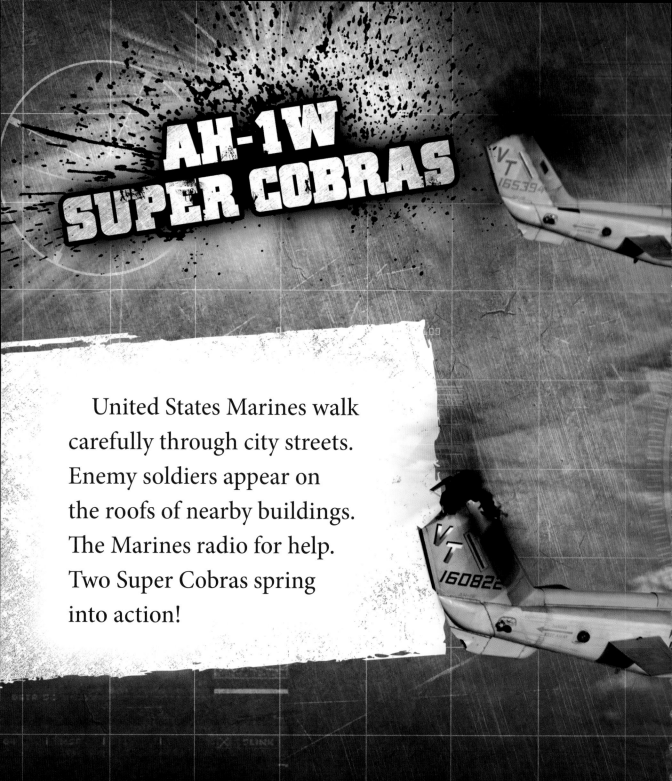

AH-1W SUPER COBRAS

United States Marines walk carefully through city streets. Enemy soldiers appear on the roofs of nearby buildings. The Marines radio for help. Two Super Cobras spring into action!

The Super Cobras enter the battle.
One fires **rockets** at the buildings.
The other fires its **machine gun**.

The enemy is defeated and the city is calm. The Super Cobras have helped the Marines complete their **mission**.

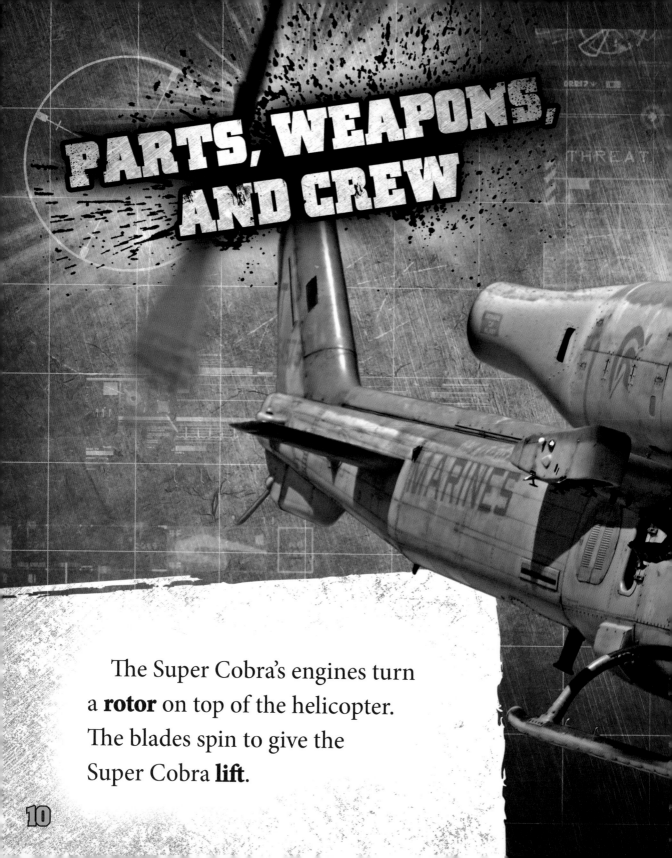

PARTS, WEAPONS, AND CREW

The Super Cobra's engines turn
a **rotor** on top of the helicopter.
The blades spin to give the
Super Cobra **lift**.

ROTOR

Super Cobra Fact

The Super Cobra has two engines. It can still fly if one engine is destroyed.

442

PILOT

CO-PILOT GUNNER

Cpl J.A. Rodriguez

CARTRIDGE ACTIVATED DEVICES

Capt N.M. "Pug" Moore

IN MEMORY OF
GYSGT "MANO" PATTON

43

Two crew members operate the Super Cobra. The pilot flies the helicopter. The **co-pilot gunner (CPG)** controls the weapons.

Super Cobra Fact

A computer connects a special lens to the machine gun. The CPG aims the gun by looking through the lens at a target.

The Super Cobra carries several rockets and **missiles**. An **infrared camera** can find enemies at night and in bad weather.

MISSILES

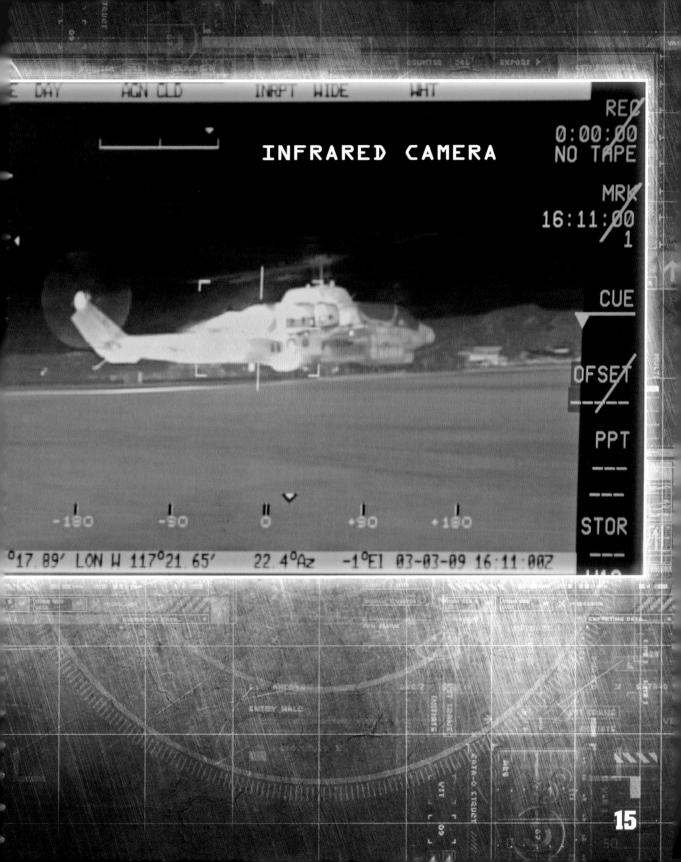

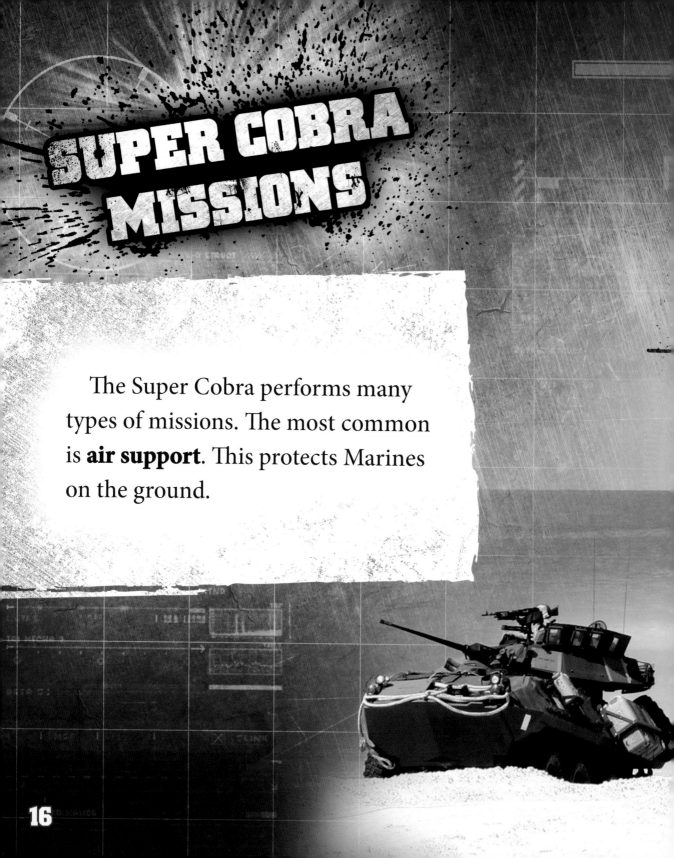

SUPER COBRA MISSIONS

The Super Cobra performs many types of missions. The most common is **air support**. This protects Marines on the ground.

Super Cobra Fact

Heavily armed Super Cobras are used to take out enemy tanks and other vehicles.

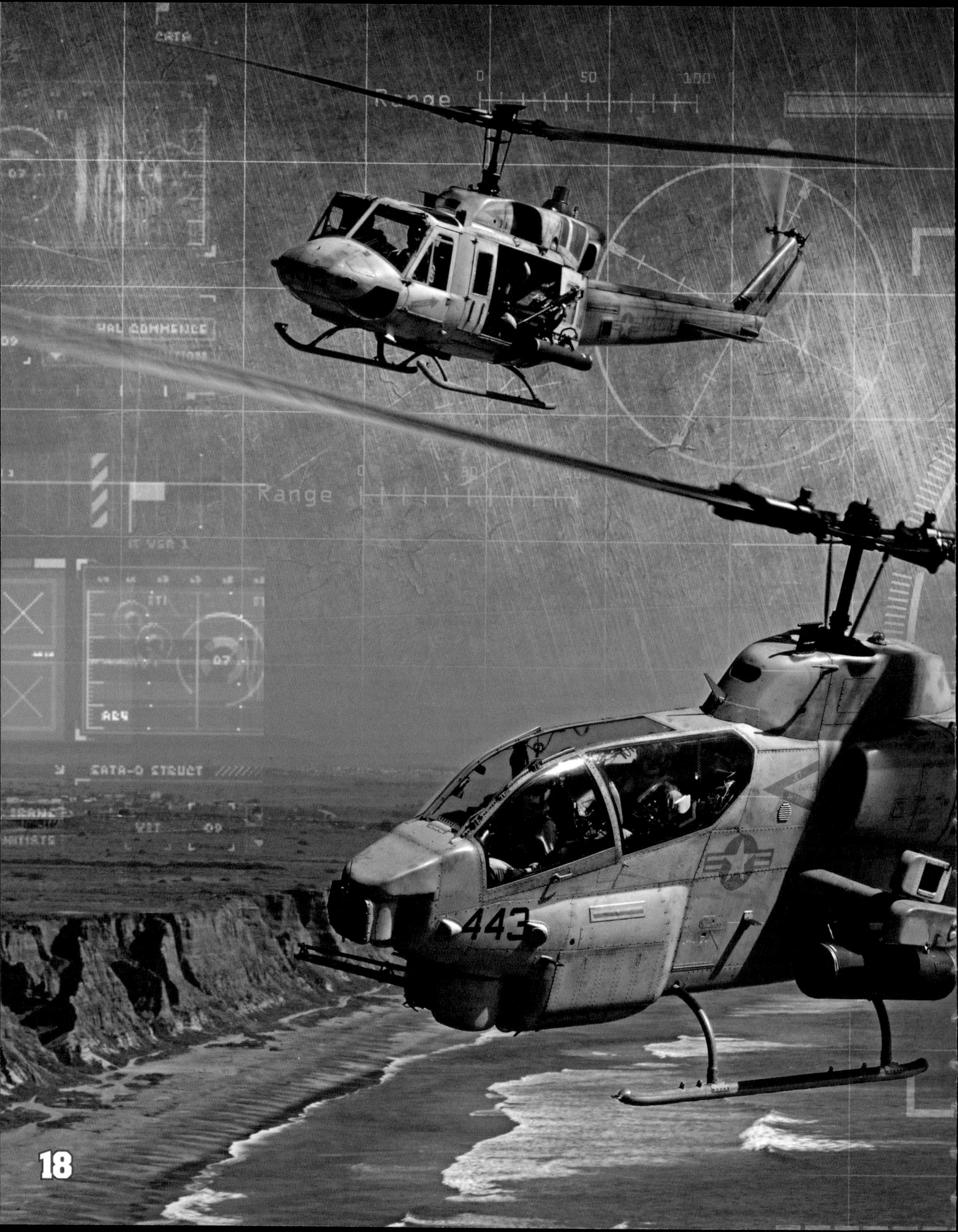
Range
0
50
100
Range
443

Super Cobras often **escort** larger helicopters that carry Marines into battle. **Recon** missions record enemy numbers and locations.

Super Cobras are very important to the United States Marine Corps. Their weapons and brave crews help complete many dangerous missions.

VEHICLE BREAKDOWN:
AH-1W SUPER COBRA

Used By:	U.S. Marine Corps
Entered Service:	1986
Length:	58 feet (17.7 meters)
Height:	14.2 feet (4.3 meters)
Rotor Diameter:	48 feet (14.6 meters)
Weight (Fully Loaded):	14,750 pounds (6,700 kilograms)
Top Speed:	218 miles (350 kilometers) per hour
Range:	403 miles (648 kilometers)
Ceiling:	18,700 feet (5,700 meters)
Crew:	2
Weapons:	machine gun, missiles, rockets
Primary Missions:	air support, escorting, recon

GLOSSARY

air support—a type of mission that involves flying close to and protecting Marines on the ground

co-pilot gunner (CPG)—the Super Cobra crew member who controls weapons and helps the pilot fly the helicopter

escort—to travel alongside and protect

infrared camera—a camera that finds the heat of other objects

lift—the force that allows a helicopter to rise off the ground

machine gun—an automatic weapon that rapidly fires bullets

missiles—explosives that are guided to a target

mission—a military task

recon—a type of mission that involves gathering information about the enemy

rockets—flying explosives that are not guided

rotor—the spinning part of a helicopter; Super Cobras have a top rotor and a tail rotor.

TO LEARN MORE

At the Library

Bodden, Valerie. *Helicopters*. Mankato, Minn.: Creative Education, 2012.

Peppas, Lynn. *Military Helicopters: Flying into Battle*. New York, N.Y.: Crabtree Pub. Co., 2012.

Von Finn, Denny. *Military Helicopters*. Minneapolis, Minn.: Bellwether Media, 2010.

On the Web

Learning more about AH-1W Super Cobras is as easy as 1, 2, 3.

1. Go to www.factsurfer.com.

2. Enter "AH-1W Super Cobras" into the search box.

3. Click the "Surf" button and you will see a list of related Web sites.

With factsurfer.com, finding more information is just a click away.

INDEX